My First Crossword Puzzle Book

by
Anna Pomaska

DOVER PUBLICATIONS, INC., New York

Published in Canada by General Publishing Company, Ltd.,
30 Lesmill Road, Don Mills, Toronto, Ontario.
Published in the United Kingdom by Constable and Company, Ltd.

My First Crossword Puzzle Book is a new work, first published
by Dover Publications, Inc., in 1990.

International Standard Book Number: 0-486-26299-5

Manufactured in the United States of America
Dover Publications, Inc.
31 East 2nd Street
Mineola, N.Y. 11501

Note

If you are about to do crossword puzzles for the first time, have no fear. The 25 puzzles in this book will be easy and fun, because you'll be able to solve them just by knowing the names of some of your favorite creatures and things!

To solve a puzzle, spell out the names of the things shown on the opposite page. The numbers next to the pictures tell you where the names belong in the puzzle. The spaces for the words run across or down; and many words cross over each other, sharing letters.

A total of four words fit into each puzzle. To get you started, we have filled in one of the words entirely, and have given at least one letter of the other three words. Notice that when we filled in one word, we automatically filled in some letters of other words that will cross over it. That's part of the way a crossword puzzle works: when you spell a word, you are rewarded with a head start in spelling another word.

After you complete a puzzle, you can check your work with the Solutions that begin on page 57. And while you're working, you can color all the pictures, too!

6

7

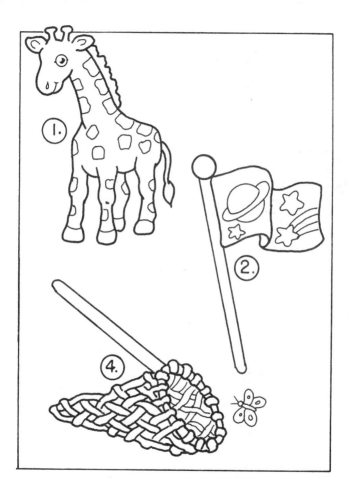

10

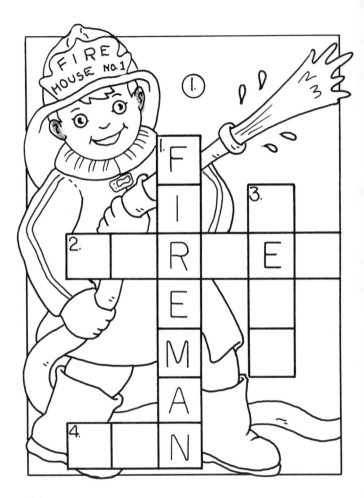

14

17

18

1. □ □ 2.C □ □ □
2. C
   □
3. Q U E E N
   □
   4.R □ □ □
   □

20

22

23

24

26

27

28

30

31

1.

2.

1. R A B B I T 3.

4. A

32

34

1.

2.

4.

1. HOUSE

3. T

36

38

2. C A S T L E

40

1. S
   Q
   U
   I
   R
   R
   E
2.
3. C
4. L

1.

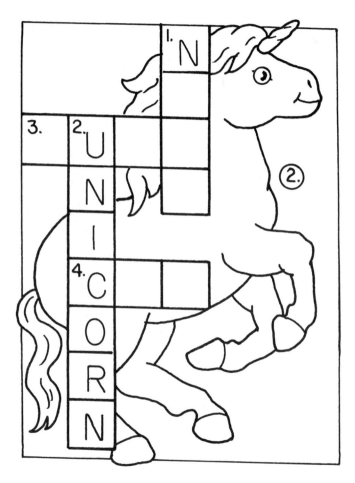

44

47

1.

3.

2.

1. A R T I S T

4. E

48

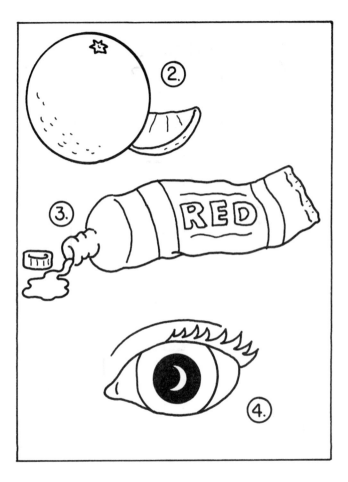

2.

3.

RED

4.

50

53

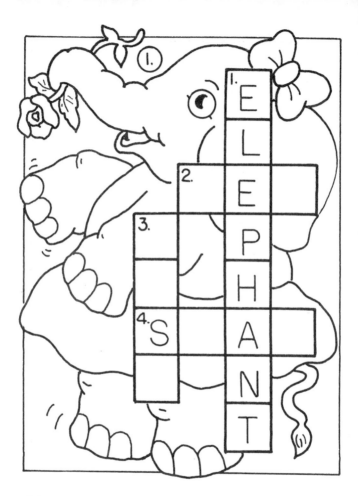

54

Solutions

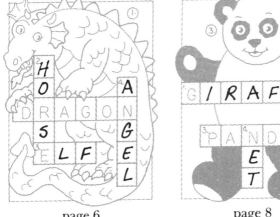

page 6

page 8

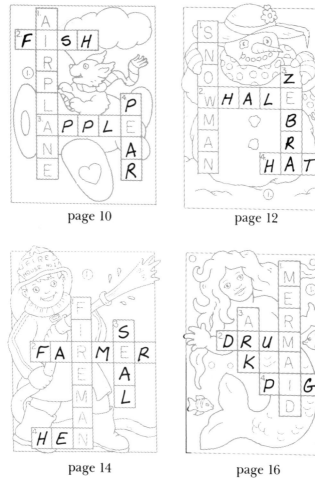

page 10

page 12

page 14

page 16

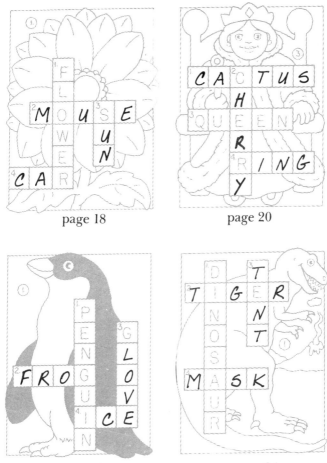

page 18

page 20

page 22

page 24

59

page 26

page 28

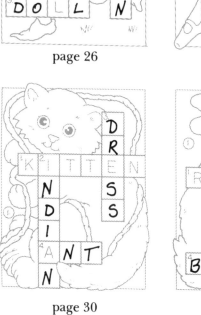

page 30

page 32

page 34

page 36

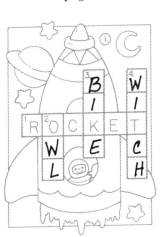

page 38

page 40

61

page 42

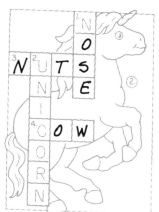

page 44

page 46

page 48

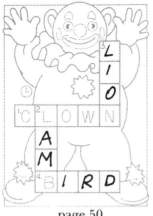

page 50

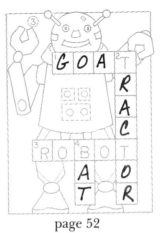

page 52

page 54